First Light, First Shadows

George Swede was born in Riga, Latvia, in 1940, and moved to Canada in 1947. A Professor Emeritus at Ryerson University, Toronto, he and his wife, the educator and writer Anita Krumins, currently divide their time between Toronto and Mexico.

Swede published his first poem in 1968 and started to focus on haiku and tanka in the 1970s and 1980s respectively. In 1977 he co-founded Haiku Canada with Eric Amann and Betty Drevniok. He has published 31 collections of poetry, and 17 other books involving children's fiction, haiku criticism, and the psychology of art and creativity.

First Light, First Shadows is his first full collection of tanka.

George Swede
First Light, First Shadows

edited by John Barlow

 Snapshot Press

First published in Great Britain in 2006 by
Snapshot Press, PO Box 132, Waterloo, Liverpool L22 8WZ

www.snapshotpress.co.uk

A catalogue record for this book
is available from the British Library

ISBN-10: 1-903543-19-3
ISBN-13: 978-1-903543-19-1

Typeset in 9/11 pt and 12/14 pt Palatino
Typeset by Molomo, Liverpool, Merseyside

Printed in Great Britain by
The Printroom (UK) Ltd, Liverpool, Merseyside

This book is printed on recyclable natural paper made from wood
grown in sustainable forests; pulps used in production are Totally
Chlorine Free (TCF)

For Anita, Juris and Andris

Acknowledgements

Thanks are due to the editors and publishers of the following publications in which present or earlier versions of many of these poems first appeared:
American Tanka, *Five Lines Down*, *Frogpond*, *Gusts*, *Hummingbird*, *Industrial Sabotage*, *New Moon: An Introduction to Issues in Contemporary American Tanka* (Redfox Press, 2001), *Poetry Nippon*, *Poets in the Classroom* (Pembroke Publishers, 1995), *red lights*, *Ribbons: Tanka Society of America Journal*, *Simply Haiku*, *Tangled Hair*, *Tanka Splendor 1990* (AHA Books, 1991), *Tanka Splendor 1997* (AHA Books, 1998), *Tanka Splendor 2003*, *The Haiku Quarterly*, *The Plaza*, *The Tanka Anthology: Tanka in English from Around the World* (Red Moon Press, 2003), *The Tanka Journal*, and *Wind Five Folded: An Anthology of English-Language Tanka* (AHA Books, 1994).

"Cold winter morning" received a Tanka Splendor Award, 1990.

"Last night I felt" was awarded 3rd Place in the Poetry Society of Japan 2nd International Tanka Contest 1990.

"Spellbound at the window" received a Tanka Splendor Award, 2003.

An earlier version of the manuscript for this book was awarded First Prize in the Snapshot Press Tanka Collection Competition 2005.

Thanks to Snapshot Press editor and publisher, John Barlow, who made many insightful suggestions that enhanced the quality of this collection.

First Light, First Shadows

Last night I felt
the first autumn chill—
or was this my way
of understanding
what you said to me?

A wife
who doesn't want me;
a dog that nips my heels—
my eyes follow
the southbound geese

Wind
and freezing rain—
I'm glad to be back
from where I left this morning
vowing never to return

Cold winter morning:
as I wait for the call
a white hair falls
from my head
and sticks to the phone

With the promotion
a corner office—
two window reflections
now vie for
my attention

Today at work
I saw the complexity
of labor versus management—
a lake gull flies silently
through the snowfall

All my learning
and I still don't know
how to make her happy—
rain ripples
my puddle face

I re-read
my brother's
suicide note—
tomatoes ripen
on the sill

Burial of a friend—
in spite of myself
I marvel at
the yellow butterfly
against the blue sky

This wild wind
heard, felt, tasted—
eyeless
a worm rises
from freshly turned earth

On the north-facing ground
that never sees the sun
still clumps of snow and ice—
things unresolved in me
make their presence known

Table jade plant
I can't know your true being
only the beauty you show—
her blue eyes, as she sips tea
are streaked with dawn

All the ideas
in these great books
you embody them
library spider, you
and your sunlit web

Spellbound at the window
the patient diagnosed
with multiple personality—
a flock of blackbirds
flying as one

Why do I need
an audience for my poems . . .
a crow caws
from the sunset-lit top
of the jack pine

A tiny cobweb
in the corner catches
the last light—
a writer of tiny poems
I leave it

I drive through rain
to an old friend
with cancer—
the windshield wiper
like a pendulum clock

A teacher for
thirty-six years, I know
even less than I thought—
the chalk dust gathered
like early snow

Last night we talked
as if we were lovers again . . .
today the snow is slush
and I watch an arthritic dog
awkwardly walking

I dance by myself
to an old favorite
on the radio—
my shadow seems
older than I

Marriage is work
work is a marriage—
such thoughts as I watch
the pair of robins
carry twigs to the maple

The Sunday crossword
with one entry done
left on the park bench . . .
the scent of spring's
first lilac blossoms

Our clothes
where they fell
on the floor
gather first light
first shadows

The neighbor
with the sharp tongue
is pregnant—
her window cactus
in full bloom

A full moon, a full tide
and a vintage red wine
yet no love—again
the words unspoken
have their say

After decades
I know her as well
as I know this red rose—
a dawn-lit dewdrop
from each thorn

Her echoing words:
"All you think of is yourself!"—
on the backyard deck
I let a mosquito
stay on my arm

Our guts
home to millions
of viruses and bacteria—
can anyone really say
"I" anymore?

The leaf-cutter ant
with its sail-shaped burden
re-crosses the tennis court—
recalling all those lost
at sea, or in their minds

Department meeting:
while the mouths utter business
the eyes ripple with
someone sailing, someone fishing
someone drowning

At dawn I enter
a street of picture windows—
showing in them all
giant trees with falling leaves
and a hunched, lone figure

A young woman
walking briskly
through the rain—
how did I notice
her tears?

Entering old age
I look less for truth
but find it more—
a mid-winter thaw reveals
pieces of sky

I awake
from the sound
of her smoker's lungs—
shadow of a bare branch
on the wall

Sharply outlined
by the first light
the spines of the cactus
and the fact of
our separate beds

The weather station says
spring begins at 3:58 p.m.
which is right now—
my reflection blurred
in the frozen puddle

She called me names
she threatened me
this woman who now
murmurs to the plants
as she waters them

A sudden burning rage
but from my lips
only a harmless cliché—
a sunbeam slants
through the dark clouds

Crossing the still pond
the water strider leaves
cobweb-thin ripples—
my life form feels
huge and graceless

Our fight over
we discuss why
we're still together—
the cat curled against
the dog's belly

Staying between
two strips of the blind
all the way across the window—
the distant gull
will never know

I don't want
to do anything
but sit and gaze—
as the ant climbs
the blade of grass sways

I can name but few
of my body's many parts,
of these many park flowers . . .
yet I live
they live

Facial massage—
I feel my skin
stretch over holes
that will soon
define me

One friend advised this
and another that—
I sit transfixed as
the weathervane points south
while the trees bend north

After the sports pages
no longer to entertainment
but to obituaries—
my pulse more visible
in each wrist

Last night she giggled
and pulled my chest hair;
nothing else happened . . .
the trees on this warm winter day
look like they should have leaves

If only years ago
I had seen myself more clearly—
the weight of many snowfalls
bends the juniper branch
to the ground

Another life
ended early for reasons
no one fathoms—
the screech
of a neighbor's saw

After the burial
I walk through the house
without turning on the lights—
a different half-moon
in each window

A hill of stones . . .
I pick up one and throw
it back in a high arc
for no reason
I can plumb

I am no more
than you
flowerbed ant—
can see no further
what's ahead

Twenty-five years
and still together
despite everything—
I let the purple thistle
stay in the garden

She's bent over
a cryptic crossword
I over a poem—
both of us lost in our
own puzzle of existence

Life's end—when, how?
Two more questions
without answers
as I watch the bee among
the fresh graveside flowers

Electrochemical
the memory of who
I am, I was—such thoughts
on the path home with a
fading flashlight beam